# My Glorious Journey

# My Glorious Journey

## FROM BAPTISM TO PRIESTLY MINISTRY

## Msgr. Theo. Joseph

| Library of Congress Control Number: | | 2011906446 |
|---|---|---|
| ISBN: | Hardcover | 978-1-4628-6123-1 |
| | Softcover | 978-1-4628-6122-4 |
| | Ebook | 978-1-4628-6124-8 |

This book was printed in the United States of America.

**To order additional copies of this book, contact:**
Xlibris Corporation
1-888-795-4274
www.Xlibris.com
Orders@Xlibris.com
98291

# Contents

# PART III—SHARED REFLECTIONS

# Thoughts

TO BE A priest means living out the gifts and the fruits of the Holy Spirit each day, each moment, and always.

A successful priest is first and foremost a holy man. This holiness precedes his priestly ordination. His priestly holiness proceeds from the gifts and fruits of the Holy Spirit received at the sacrament of confirmation. All are born from the "born-again" experience at Baptism.

# Preface

MY SUSPICION PEAKED when my medical doctor proposed, in fact highly recommended, that I have consultations with an oncologist. The meaning and implications of this recommendation meant that my medical doctor had a suspicion of cancer but wanted to verify it.

Trembling with fear, I visited the oncologist, and after a battery of tests, it was confirmed that I was a cancer patient. Wow, I thought to myself, my death warrant is signed and sealed but not yet delivered. My preparation for death had begun, and for the very first time, it dawned on me that death was not too far away. The first step in this preparation was to fight death and fight it with all the ammunition at my disposal.

I will not and cannot give up without a fight. I have read in the Bible that the last enemy to be destroyed was death. True, that is my last enemy. The others I have fought, and thanks be to God, I have not been defeated. Now this last enemy has shown itself and must be destroyed as well.

I did not ask the oncologist too many questions. I had to prepare for war, the fiercest war in my history, a war of life over death, a war that will take me from here to eternity. I could not give up or allow fear to paralyze me. I decided to do everything the doctors asked of me: to face surgery bravely, to face radiation therapy bravely, to face the discomforts of being awakened several times during the night, and to face the fatigue I felt during the day as part of the warfare.

Then one day, it hit me. Why don't I write a book entitled *A Glorious Journey* as part of my war against the enemy called death? By facing off with death I can win, for I will look at death in the face and punch it in the nose. Death will have no power over me. That book will be helpful to others in their defeat of death. It can and has been done.

*A Glorious Journey* is my appreciation of life.

Do not expect this to be an autobiography or even a biography. Do not expect this to be a mea culpa exposé of all that I have done wrong. I have already done this in the confessional as St. James told us that we must confess our sins to one another. This is a sharing of the high points in my life—high points that I am extremely proud of and high points from which you can grow as you step out in faith.

# My Focus

AS A PERSON who shares the experience of celebrating life, I aim to do my best to be the following:

## To be

A person with freedom and integrity,
Clean of thought and true of heart,
Strong of will, responsible, and self-reliant,
To make a personal commitment for my life, and
To be constant and true to my word.

Ready to serve others,
Involved with my community,
Defender of other people's rights,
Pledged to democracy and committed to development,
A lover of justice and promoter of peace,
To value human labor,
To build a family on love, and
To be aware of my own dignity
And that of others.
Thoughtful and creative,
To leave the world better than I found it,
To strive for the integrity of the natural world,

Learning continually and searching
For paths still unexplored,
To do my work well
To be free from the hunger to possess,
And independent of material things.
Open to God through prayer
To have a transcendental sense of celebrating life,
To reach out to God,
To live my faith joyfully
And make it part of daily life,
To be open to dialogue and understanding,
And to respect the religious beliefs of others.

*Amen.*

# PART I

# From Physical Birth to Rebirth

MARCH 23, 1948, was a very bright spring day. The sun was rising slowly in the sky, and the clouds were playing their game of "hide and seek" with the sun. A Zephyr was blowing from the east, and the leaves of the trees were all dancing to symphony created by the wind. People were rushing to and fro among the shops, purchasing bread and other items for breakfast to prepare the children for school.

The religious atmosphere was somber since it was Tuesday in the Holy Week. The women's and men's retreats were over, and the priests were resting from the long lines of confessions that they heard over the past two weeks. They were celebrating their Holy Week free day, shopping and relaxing in the city. That was the day which was chosen for me to be born. I was in quite a hurry to get out of entombment in the womb. I was in quite a hurry to see the light of day, which I heard of while in the womb. I was in quite a hurry to see the face whose voice I heard each day and many times each day. I was in quite a hurry to escape the loneliness of that womb and to be truly a part of the natural world.

When I finally escaped from the womb, it was my moment of grace, my moment of freedom, my moment of deliverance. I let the world know that I was free. Before the midwife could spank me, I was screaming, "Freedom, freedom, freedom, freedom! Never again will I enter this womb of loneliness and of imprisonment." I understood why Nicodemus asked Jesus if it were possible to enter his mother's womb and be born a second time. Not Nicodemus! He was free from the womb, and even if it were possible to return, he did not wish to remain in the womb. He wanted to be freed from the entombment of that womb. Freedom! Freedom! Freedom!

That spring day was my moment of sucking human food from my mother's breast. For nine long months I dreamt of being fully human and fully alive out of my mother's womb. The moment arrived. Freedom! Freedom! Freedom! Thank God for that freedom. Thank God I am born. Thanks, Mom, you have set me free.

For nine months, I heard my mother's voice. I heard her praying. I heard her singing. Sometimes I felt she sang too much. "How much is that dog in the window, bow, bow?" I felt her anger sometimes. I felt her pain at times. Sometimes I caused her pain when I was at play with the vessels and the umbilical cord and did kick her very much. My kicking convinced her that I was a boy, and she prepared anxiously for my arrival.

If all mothers were like my mother, then each birth would be an experience of love, of delight, of surprise and sometimes of depression. The expectation and the "homecoming" was, for my mother, a delightful experience. I understood why people refer to pregnant women as "expecting."

# Born Again

JESUS TOLD NICODEMUS that a person must be born again of water and the Holy Spirit. Now that I was born of flesh, I had to be "born again." I did not, could not, and would not go back to the womb, which had freed me. Although I was surrounded by amniotic fluid in the womb and breathed like a fish, I wanted to be reborn through water and the Holy Spirit and breathe God's fresh air and be held by my mother as she ensured that I was fed, burped, and held close to her heart.

While I lay on my mother's bed at home, my mother was making arrangements with her family for my born-again experience. She loved one of her brothers and asked him to be my godfather. What a privilege it was for him, but he declined. To this day, I cannot understand why he declined, but he proposed his wife's brother-in-law as my godfather. He was a tailor by profession and agreed. I still do not know why her brother declined.

My godmother was chosen before I was born. Her name is Mita. She was a source of strength for me and my mother. She understood very well her role as my godmother. She considered me very special and treated me that way. As a mother herself, she knew some of the secrets of child-rearing, which my mother did not know. Thus she was my mother's teacher as well as my teacher on my way to humanization.

The day of my being "born again" came within one month of my physical birth. As was the custom at the time, I had quite a procession for my born-again moment. My godparents, one or two cousins, and my "da" (nanny), dressed in the traditional St. Lucian dress (duiette) carried me from our home to the church, a distance of about two hundred yards. That movement was also my epiphany, since many of the neighbors came out to see and make comments as neighbors often do. "He looks like his mother." "He has the nose of his father." "He has the length of his grandfather." No one said, "He looks unique. He looks like himself." No one gave me gifts of gold, frankincense, and myrrh. I remember one lady saying, "He looks like his mother. He will be lucky." In fact, that lady repeated this more than once as I grew up. She reminded me all the time that she had said these words before my baptism. Was her name "Prophetess Anna" or the "Priest Simeon"?

It was early afternoon when we arrived at the church. That day was very warm, and my baptism robe, though made from fine cotton, was unbearably hot. I began to demand my freedom from those unbearable clothes by crying out loud, freedom, freedom, freedom! My "da" (nanny) began to rock me to allow the breeze to cool me down. My godparents were uncomfortable with my cry for freedom. I am sure I was neither hungry nor thirsty. I only wanted to be free from that long and uncomfortable baptismal robe.

I had no name up to this point; everyone called me "baby" or "baba," but I was given a name as part of my baptism. My godfather named me Theophilus, a name that he had read from the Acts of the Apostles and Gospel of St. Luke. The baptizing priest gave me the name Théophile, the French to the Greek Theophilus. My godmother gave me the name Anthony after her favorite saint, Anthony of Padua. My personhood took shape. I was born again, baptized, made a catholic, and had to listen and respond to a new name, Theophilus Anthony. For some reason, Anthony soon became Tony, a name I had to respond to as I was being humanized. The actual baptism, the pouring of the water, was a quiet event. I had sounded my freedom cry for so long that I had no scream in me again. The cold water was poured on my head and Fr. Sevienne said, "I baptize you in the name of the Father and of the Son and of the Holy Spirit." My "da" (nanny) and godmother held the belief that if I screamed when the water touched my forehead, I would have a very good voice, but I was too tired and too exhausted to scream. I just wanted a quiet and cool cradle to lie and sleep.

The procession back home was uneventful since I was asleep. When I awoke, I was home in my mother's arms, who called me by name for the first time. Of course, she had to ask my godparents to tell her my name. For many days she would forget my name and was always asking others what my name was. I am sure there were times when I felt like belting out my name to her. At the age of one month, I knew my name and my mother did not, but such are the facts of life.

The baptism ceremony was over, and it was time to party. We had a gramophone or a phonograph and a very large collection of long-playing records. All my uncles and aunts were present for the party. While I lay asleep, they were having a party. After all, it was my baptism, and I was not at my own party. Be it as it may, I was a born-again Christian, and no one could take that away from me. I died with Christ, and I rose with him to new life. From henceforth, I am a Christian and a catholic—freedom, freedom, freedom!

There were many people in my household Philomene Barthelmy (Ma B), Bernadette Servais (Dedette), Joan and Linus, my godmother's children, Mita or Nenen, my godmother, and my mother—quite a household of all those persons. I was the baby and the center of attention.

# Humanization

AFTER A RATHER lavish celebration of my born-again life, there was a quiet time, an uneventful three years, in which I was being humanized—"come," "go," "don't touch," "if you cannot hear, you must feel," "sit down" or "scram." My name was called well over sixty times per day for various reasons. One of the reasons was to "come for prayer." It was more exciting to be out of the house than to be in the house. It was more exciting to look out of the window than to look at the cross and statues of the saints and the Blessed Mother on our family altar.

My godsister, Joan, a pupil teacher at the St. Aloysius Roman Catholic Boys' Infant School, decided that I should accompany her to school each day. From age three, I had to be in school from 9:00 a.m. to 12:00 p.m. and from 1:30 p.m. to 3:00 p.m. After the morning session, we walked home for lunch and returned for the afternoon session. Needless to say, I did get my beauty sleep in the principal's office. Her name was Ms. Joseph, and she came from the same village as my family.

"Sister" Joan, as I called her, was an outdoors person. She was involved in the Girl Guides and the Catholic Youth Organization. I remember some Girl Guides who made me their excuse when their meetings were boring.

For two years, my life was taken over by "Sister Joan." She took me to Girl Guide camps, to Girl Guide meetings, to teachers' conferences, to CYO meetings, to choir rehearsals, etc. I truly enjoyed those activities. I was the only male, and those women made me the center of their attention and the focus of their love and goodness. I did not mind at all.

There was a time, I recall, that I was sent to a preschool run by another lady from Choiseul, who lived at Morne Avette (Rose Hill). Ms. Prisca was her name. I believe that was before Sister Joan began to take me to school with her.

I began formal education when I was four years old, at the St. Aloysius RC Boys' Infant School. The only difference was that I had to wear the school uniform and I was separated from Joan. Many a time, my class teacher had to come to Joan's class to get me.

# Yes

ONE CENTRAL PART of our Catholic life is the reception of Holy Communion. In baptism, God accepted me since I was baptized in the name of the Father, the Son and the Holy Spirit. In Holy Communion, I received Jesus as he gave himself to me. The preparation for that event was long and at times frightful. From age seven to age eight, I had to learn my catechism, learn my catholic prayers, prepare to receive the Sacrament of Reconciliation, go to the tailor (my godfather) for measurement of my lily-white suit. It was a very stressful year for me and the members of my family. My grandfather, all my aunts and uncles, Joan's friends, and my godmother's friends were all anxious about my first Communion. Leading the anxious brigade was my mother.

Some of the children in the neighborhood were also preparing to receive their First Holy Communion. I remember a young boy of my age living in the neighborhood, Vincent Gilbert. He was my best friend. He has gone to meet the Lord. May he rest in peace.

We had a test to find out how well we knew our catechism. The priest was the examiner. My examiner was Fr. Charles Jesse, FMI, an assistant priest at the cathedral. I was trembling with fear as I was led to that priest for questioning. First question was—"Who made you?" Second question—"Recite the confiteor." And the third question—"What is the sacrament of the Holy Eucharist?" I answered all the questions haltingly, afraid that the white priest was a monster waiting to devour me. We just did not trust white people, but we respected them. After answering the questions, I was given a ticket to take home. I had passed. The other areas of preparation could be put in place.

When I took the ticket home, there was great joy, so much joy that everyone was in tears. I never understood tears of joy. Everybody was proud of me. My mother and godmother told the whole world that I was "in First Holy Communion."

The date for First Holy Communion was April 12, 1956, just after my eighth birthday and just before my eighth anniversary of baptism. The preparation was extensive. My aunt in a village gave a sheep to be slaughtered for the occasion. My other family members and Joan's friends and others chipped in for my First Holy Communion. My godfather gave me the white suit. One of my mother's friends on the French Island of Martinique sent me the white shoes. My haircut was from Staffy Odlum, and the cakes were from other friends. In fact, I had three cakes. One was in the shape of a book with a beautiful golden rosary and a cross and was given by my mother's employer. I had many gifts of prayer books, rosaries, holy cards, etc.

# Reconciliation

WEDNESDAY, APRIL 11, was Reconciliation Day for those of us preparing for First Holy Communion. I was thoroughly prepared for this sacrament by my teachers at the school and more so by my godmother, who explained to me the nature of sin, the payment of sin, and grace of the sacrament. She taught me how I should confess in general terms. The particulars, I had to decide for myself.

At first, I thought that the formula for confession was the most important part of the sacrament. Thus I memorized the formula carefully.

"Bless me, Father, for I have sinned. I accuse myself of . . ." You listen to the priest and answer truthfully whatever questions he may ask you, and then you recite the "Act of Contrition," listen to the penance the priest gives, then leave the confessional, and do your penance.

My turn came for confession, and I went to the confession box. I was confident, for I had rehearsed the formula over and over again. I said the entire formula, but forgot to say my sins. The priest gently reminded me that I forgot to say my sins. I remembered that I panicked at that moment, and after a period of silence that was actually shorter than it seemed, I slowly began to say my sins, careful not to forget any. I think this first confession was my best confession for this part of my life. I left the confessional feeling free and properly forgiven, never more to sin again, but more importantly, to "carefully avoid the occasions of sin."

After confession, the way home was quiet. My aunt accompanied me home. At home, I was not allowed to leave the house for the balance of that day. I spent most of the time with my simple prayer book, memorizing the prayers before and after Holy Communion and other prayers, which my family thought I should learn. My entertainment were the Bible stories, which Joan read to me to convince me of who Jesus is and the role he plays in my life, especially when my soul is cleansed from sin. I remember Joan telling me that only the "pure in heart will see God," and I knew that I had made a good confession and that my heart was as pure as it was after my born-again experience. It was the moment when I really wanted to see God, to go to heaven. But I had not received Jesus in Holy Communion. It was not yet time to die and see Jesus. I was just beginning to live and be with Jesus.

# First Holy Communion

THE MORNING OF April 12 was another spring day. I remembered I was born on a spring day, baptized on a spring day, and now I was receiving my first Holy Communion on a spring day. Like the day of my physical birth and the day when I was born again, the day was beautiful. Dressed in my lily-white suit, I walked to the school for the procession to the church.

The people in the neighborhood all turned out to see the procession of the children on their way to church, commenting on how we were dressed. The girls were dressed in their long dresses and veils as though getting prepared for marriage. The girls from the neighborhood all looked so beautiful that I had to look well to recognize Sandra, Catherine, Jill, Margaret, and many others.

On arrival at the school, the Sisters of St. Joseph of Cluny of Ireland and various teachers, together with Ms. Catherine Joseph, the principal of the Infant School, all dressed in their Sunday best, were organizing us in lines for the procession. We were not allowed to talk with each other, but I talked with my eyes as I looked at all my friends, looking very holy as though they had seen a vision. The procession began slowly to the church. It lasted for about twenty-five minutes.

On arrival at the church, the Mass began. We were onlookers, not participants. I was guessing when Jesus would come from heaven to the altar. I think I missed that moment, for when I blinked, Jesus had already come. I felt a little disappointed, since there was so much I had to say to Jesus when he came. Anyway, I was told that I could speak to Jesus when I received him in Holy Communion, but I was afraid to speak with him then as I would be so concerned about the host touching my teeth and remaining on my tongue until it was dissolved, that my attention would not be where I wanted it to be.

The time had come; the moment was here. I was led to the altar; I knelt down with my hand covered with the altar rail cloth. The priest went from east to west along the altar rails, saying, as he went from person to person, "Corpus Christi." When he came to me, I could have fainted with fear. Here I am, and here is Jesus. I felt my heart was beating in my chest. Although it was a cool spring day, I was sweating. Thank God the priest was quick, and I returned to my seat before I could faint.

It was a joyous time; parents, friends, and relatives were all together, perhaps for the first time. After the celebration, I was hungry, since according to church law, I had to fast from midnight and could not drink a cup of tea or even water before receiving Holy Communion. Food eluded me since I had to go to the Botanical Gardens for pictures, after which we went home. I had a breakfast fit for a king: cocoa tea, bakes, bread, and eggs. It was truly a good breakfast. I was kissed and kissed and kissed. What a sense of freedom my First Holy Communion gave to me!

But the day was not over. At 3:00 p.m., we had to be back in church to formally renounce. I said it, and I meant it.

I renounce the devil
And all his works and pomps,
And I give myself to Jesus
Through the hands of Mary.

That was truly a climax to a time of celebration. I was able to call God, "Abba," from my baptism. Now I could call Jesus, "Brother." I was baptized in the name of the Trinity and today, the second person came to live in me. I gave myself to him through his mother and my mother, Mary. What an experience! What a revelation!

The hymn "Long Ago, I Made Faith's Solemn Vow" became truly my prayer and my renewal.

Long ago, I made faith's solemn vow,
But my sponsors then lent me their voice;
I renew all my promises now,
And I do this of my own free choice.

I renew all promises now,
And I do this of my own free choice

I believe then in God, Three-in-One,
And will seal this belief with my blood.
Feeble reason, the victory is won!
Nor shall Faith by thy pride be withstood.

I renew all promises now,
And I do this of my own free choice

I believe God came down from above,
To seek man and to save lost mankind.
And His Bride, Mother Church, I do love,
Yes, I love Her with heart and with mind.

I renew all promises now,
And I do this of my own free choice.

# Yes to Yes

I HAVE SO far journeyed from pre-birth to birth to rebirth to giving me to Jesus through Mary. Now my journey continues to the next step in my Catholic initiation: my confirmation. I did not fully understand what confirmation did. All I knew was that it lacked the pomp and majesty of First Holy Communion. The catechism was harder and so was the pass mark. Added to that, the school work got harder, and there was an excitement about going to the only Catholic secondary school for boys.

Fr. Joseph Vrignaud, FMI, the vicar general and parish priest of the capital city of Castries, St. Lucia, was my examiner. One question I remembered he asked was, "What must you do to inherit eternal life?"

I answered, "I must follow the rule of life taught by Jesus Christ." I rattled it out. The other questions were not so exciting. I had passed the examination for confirmation. I was now eleven years old. The confirmation date was set for November, and the first bishop of Castries, Charles Gachet, FMI, would be the celebrant.

An interesting thought about confirmation is the fact that my birth, rebirth, and First Holy Communion were all in the spring or in the months of dry weather, but my confirmation, the last of the sacraments of my initiation, was in the autumn or the rainy season. What is God saying to me? Later on, it will be observed that Bishop Charles, who anointed me with chrism at my confirmation, is the same bishop who will anoint me with chrism at my ordination eighteen years later (1974), only this time, in the spring.

It felt good to be a confirmed Catholic, as the sacrament had thrown me into the realm of maturity. I was responsible and more accountable to God and to his Church for all my actions and inactions. It was as though after being a confirmed Catholic, God was always watching me. Where can I hide that God will not find me? What can I do that God will not see me? What can I say that God will not hear me? Perhaps I will do everything right, then God will not have to bother with me. But God says he loves me and will pursue me because of that love. How can I, as a confirmed Catholic, love God back? That was a tough time in my life after confirmation.

It was tough in other ways. I was entering a new phase in my physiological life, a new stage in my intellectual life, a new stage in my psychological life, and a new stage in my spiritual life. As a confirmed Christian now, I had to believe what Jesus said, "Behold! I have come to make all things new." All things included me. I had made my personal commitment to Jesus as I went through the changes in my life. Jesus is making me new. I am being renewed. That was the most trying part of my life. I had to be new. The old Theophilus had to die so that the new Theophilus, renewed by Christ, could emerge to new life, from the cocoon to become a butterfly.

# Confirmation to Ordination

VERY FEW PERSONS understand that new life. I did not understand it. Like physical birth, something in me had to be freed. It was frightening and at times humiliating. I had to explain or try to explain to many persons what that new life meant. I was a different person in the eyes of many people, but in my own eyes, I felt I was the same. Confirmation, with its seven gifts and twelve fruits, was reshaping my life. Why don't all confirmed Catholics have the same experience of personal renewal? Was I chosen especially by God for that experience? I have no idea. All I know is I was walking with my God. Prayer began to be a constant in that period of my life. Bible reading was another area. Those two renewals set me on the path to walk with God. Needless to say, there were times when God was walking too fast, and there were times when I was walking too fast. With time, I learnt the footsteps of my God. "Left, right, right, right, left, right, left, left, about-turn, quick march, slope arms, shoulder arms, trail arms, at ease, attention." I had to learn from God in order to follow God.

The Lord marched me through the seminary of St. John Vianney in Trinidad. For seven years, I marched; sometimes I stopped, sometimes I walked, and sometimes I doubted. In fact, oftentimes, I doubted especially those moments when I felt that I was marching alone. Whenever the doubts arose, the Lord turned me around—"About-turn, about-turn." In those about-turns, the

Lord was always setting new areas of growth before me. On one such occasion, he led me to the Chest Hospital in Caura, Trinidad, where I met a young man called Daniel Webster. I watched his condition deteriorate but prayed with and for him. Within four months, Daniel Webster was dead. I thanked God that I was able to meet with him and to be there for his mother, father, and younger brother. It does seem to me that as I walked as best as I could with the Lord, he was giving me the opportunity to sharpen my pastoral skills. I could not see it at the time, but now I see what amazing grace is all about. Even when I felt lost, Jesus was finding me.

As the date of my priestly ordination grew nearer and nearer, I began to panic. I questioned myself and questioned God. Is that what I should be? Did my confirmation affect me so much that my eyes were foggy and I was escaping from reality, trying to find solace in the priesthood? The decision was really tough, but I felt that I could not turn back. I was caught in a world of doubt and a world of certainty. There were times when all I could say was, "Father, take this cup away from me." Then I would pause and say, "Let thy will, not mine, be done."

The night before the ordination was my night of struggle, like Jacob, who struggled with the angel. I could not and did not sleep. The struggle was on. Did I need exorcism at that stage? I prayed for daylight. I prayed for the hour of ordination to come and go. I knew what it took to struggle with God and for God. After the ceremony of ordination, I had quite a headache, the aftereffects of my struggle that night, May 25, 1974. I never had such a struggle again. Thank God.

I am of the opinion that God was happy. I did his will even when I had doubts. I believe the seven gifts and twelve fruits that

I received at confirmation were God's gift to me for his Church. They have been there for my use as I encounter God daily.

I understood life as a continuum from physical birth to spiritual rebirth, from receiving Jesus in the sacraments of reconciliation and Holy Eucharist to receiving the Holy Spirit in the sacrament of confirmation and to continue walking step by step with God. That is true freedom. I understood that there are three certainties in life: God is, I am, and Today is. All others are propositions and desires of the heart. I understood that to walk with the certainty of who God is, is to be certain of who I am, packed with propositions and uncertainties.

The Sacrament of Holy Orders opened new possibilities for me. In that sacrament, all the gifts and the fruits of the Holy Spirit had to be evident in my life. The born-again experience is a true relationship with God through Jesus in the Holy Spirit. I was called in a special way to live out the seven gifts and the twelve fruits, opening each as needed.

Ordination did not cure me of doubt or uncertainties; rather, it put order in my doubts. Ordination, or the Sacrament of Holy Orders, allowed me the grace to put order in my doubts and strength in my certainties. Ordination was not for me a sacrament of choice between marriage and celibacy. I never chose either. I chose Christ, and Christ chose me. Like Moses, as long as I kept my hands lifted toward heaven, I was winning. Thank God for the many persons who were willing to prop up my hands each time they began sagging from fatigue.

Celibacy, which to date is an integral part of Holy Orders, is not being opposed to marriage. Oftentimes, one has that opinion, an either-or proposition. My experience tells me that they complement each other. To put it simply, if I can be a very good husband and father, I can also be a very good celibate, and if I can be a very good celibate, I can also be a very good husband and father. Whatever the sacrament, be it Holy Orders or matrimony, one must keep one's eyes fixed on Jesus. One must not lose focus. Jesus is the prize. In the race of faith, one must be totally and completely committed to live out the seven gifts and twelve fruits that one receives at confirmation.

Just as confirmation is a process of becoming because one must live out God's gifts, ordination is also a process that allows me a daily encounter with Jesus, who encounters me in the celebration of the official prayers of the church and the daily celebration of the Eucharist.

In the Eucharist, I discovered both who I am, a born-again Catholic, and what I am, a born-again Catholic ordained priest.

# A Work in Progress

ORDINATION DOES NOT make one a priest. Rather, as I mentioned earlier, it is a sacrament that allows the Holy Spirit to order the gifts and the fruits bestowed on us at baptism and confirmation. I am becoming a priest, or as some said, I am a work in progress.

The seminary educated me in such subjects as philosophy, theology, sociology, psychology, epistemology, logic, use of English, comparative religion, and canon law, but it did not prepare me to be a priest, nor did I learn what a priest really is. I suppose that was left for me to discover in the years after ordination. The subjects I studied were the tools to help in that discovery, and life's experience would enable me in that regard. What a priest does was easy. I saw priests in action, dispensing the sacraments, visiting the sick, and managing the parish finances—in fact, being the chief executive officer in a parish and ensuring that the weekly collections are always on the upswing. For some reason, I wanted to define my priesthood differently. All that a priest does was good, since it both defined and described his role in the parish community, but it did not tell me who a priest is.

# To Be or Not to Be

I WAS TORN between being a religious or a secular priest. I feared the politics involved in joining a mostly white, French, and missionary community on an island that was preparing itself to throw off the yoke of political dependence and to accept being independent. I felt the tension between the FMI (sons of Mary Immaculate) from Vendée in France and the burgeoning Afro-St. Lucian clergy, most of whom were assigned to the cathedral parish. My thought was that Bishop Charles Gachet, FMI, wanted a black church with a white face.

That should not be seen as a criticism of Bishop Charles Gachet; rather, he was trying his best to cope with the changing environment of St. Lucia and St. Lucians, who were defining themselves as Afro-St. Lucians, influenced by the black-power revolution in the United States and in Trinidad and Tobago. "Black and proud" was the theme and the feeling of many persons, including the Afro-St. Lucian priests.

I truly admired Bishop Charles Gachet and the FMI fathers. They were in the majority. They belonged to a religious foreign missionary community. They recognized that with time, the St. Lucian diocesan church would emerge and begin to define itself within the St. Lucian culture. They realized that they had to begin their departure structures in order to open the way of the St. Lucian diocesan clergy. It was sad to see them go, but that was the only way the St. Lucian Church would grow. Their work was complete.

On my part, I was an active observer of a pregnant church in labor pains waiting to give birth to its own. The birthing process, though difficult, could not be aborted but had to proceed as God had planned. Seminary studies did not prepare me for this. I had to rely on the Holy Spirit whom I received at baptism, confirmation, and ordination to give me the fortitude to use the various gifts that life's situations demanded.

In the process of becoming a priest, I had the privilege to work with several bishops. All those bishops worked with the clergy and the college of consulters. Bishop Charles Gachet, FMI, assigned me to the Parish of the Assumption, Vieux-Fort (South). Archbishop Patrick Webster, OSB, assigned me to the parish of St. Phillip and St. James and then to the Assumption Parish in Soufriere (West). Bishop Richard Lester Guilly, S. J., apostolic administrator, assigned me to Fatima Parish, La Clery (Castries). Archbishop Kelvin Felix assigned me to the Cathedral Parish (1985-2002) and to the parish of St. Peter East (2002-2009).

Each of these bishops brought me ever closer to defining my priesthood, but each definition seemed to lack something. I knew that I was not merely a social worker, yet my ministry involved social work. I knew I was neither a psychologist nor psychotherapist, yet my ministry involved both those disciplines. My ministry involved prayer: prayer for myself and prayer for others. In defining the task of an apostle (Mark 3:13), Jesus said, "I want you to be with me." That is the essence of the priesthood, being with Jesus. That is what defines me and gives meaning to my priesthood. In fact, it gives meaning to my life. The first thing I remember as a child is learning to pray. At every stage of my life, prayer was the catalyst. The last thing I hope to do before I die is pray.

The gift of being able to pause and pray, no matter what the circumstances or the conditions, is truly a gift from the Holy Spirit, and it brings healing to myself and others. In the following chapter, as I continue about becoming a priest, I will share some of the highlights of my ministry to God's people, which is part of my becoming the priest that God wants me to be.

# PART II

## Ministry in Action with Jesus

# God at Work

## a)  Gladina's Story

JESUS CHRIST IS Lord and Savior of us all. I feel privileged to share with you what the Lord is doing through the ministry that he has allowed me to share with his church. The ministry of inner healing is not as spectacular as the ministry of physical healing or the ministry of deliverance, yet the ministry of inner healing is as important for the Church and for the world.

Before I give scriptural bases for the ministry of inner healing, I want to share with you what I believe was the moment when I felt the Lord calling me from the ministry of physical healing and deliverance to the ministry of inner healing.

Many years ago, at a charismatic conference, I was drawn to the workshops for healing. I saw the Lord work many miracles that day, and I felt very happy that so many came to that workshop and so many left healed. There was one person, however, who was not healed. She came to us on her wheelchair, and we prayed for her. That was the big miracle I would like to see: the paralyzed woman being able to walk. I did pray the prayer of faith. I knew that Jesus promised that whatever we ask in faith, we would receive, but the woman could not stand up on her own. Some persons would help her up, but she would slump right down in her chair.

Something was wrong. Some other brothers and sisters in the ministry of the word of wisdom and word of knowledge came over to us. It was revealed through them that the lady of the wheelchair, whom we shall call "Gladina" was not letting go of something—some hurt—that she had been nursing for many years. She had nursed that hurt for so long that she became an addict—addicted to the hurt she had held on to all these years.

I had never met a "hurt addict." I have met and prayed with drug addicts, alcoholics, and workaholics, but a "hurtaholic" I had never met. Gladina's story is one that shows the addiction to hurt when love turns sour.

Gladina was married to the love of her live, Tompat. They made plans together and their material wealth gave them both a sense of material security. Oh, how they loved each other! Many times during the day, they would call each other, just to say hello. That was an ideal marriage.

One Sunday afternoon, Gladina and Tompat left home for a cool drive. As they approached an intersection, a truck ran into their vehicle. Gladina was pinned to the passenger side of the vehicle and had to be rushed to the hospital. Tompat walked away with only a few scratches. Gladina suffered a paralysis from the waist down. After many months of therapy, Gladina did not improve. She became more and more depressed and blamed Tompat for her misery. She became less and less physically attractive to Tompat, and little by little, a chasm developed between them. Tompat began to come home from work later and later. He lost the romantic relationship with Gladina. Finally, he stopped coming home. The marriage broke. Tompat sought a divorce and left Gladina.

Gladina felt the pain of separation from Tompat. She grieved over her accident in which she lost the ability to walk. She grieved over the fact that all the plans she had made would not be fulfilled. She grieved over the fact that Tompat had left. Her grief turned into anger and resentment, almost bordering on hate. She wished the worse for Tompat and his new wife. As time went by, the feelings of anger and resentment did not get any better. In fact, she nursed those feelings and had always expressed the fact that she could never forgive Tompat.

While nursing those feelings, Gladina was also seeking physical healing. She read the scriptures and felt that the Lord would make her walk again. She was not willing to let go. She was willing to keep on carrying Tompat, whose weight made it impossible for her to stand up and walk. Gladina needed "inner healing."

I left Gladina sitting in her wheelchair. I realized that perhaps we should journey with her through her life, especially at the historical moment when Tompat left her. I felt that, although that may take much time, I should be able to give that time to slowly help her come face-to-face with the hurt—confront the hurt, forgive Tompat, and free herself from that excess baggage.

Let me add that Gladina had gone into counseling, but she was not prepared to let go. It was so comfortable to live in the world of hate, planning at each moment the kind of revenge she would take and hating the fact that another woman was having the joy and happiness with Tompat that she had hoped to have.

Since that experience, "inner healing" has formed a central part of my ministry to God's people. I had to minister to myself first of all. I had to search within me for any excess baggage and heavy persons that I was carrying. I had to discover the areas of my life when I experienced hurt. I had to be able to reach deep within me and forgive me and those whom I had avoided, living or dead. I also had to develop the "I am sorry" attitude to all those whom I caused hurt, knowingly and unknowingly. I developed the prayer of forgiveness and have used that prayer for my ministry. I had to recognize myself (to use the words of Henry Nouwen) as a wounded healer. It was important for me to minister to myself, for as I ministered to others and brought them through the various stages of their lives, it was easy for me to be so sympathetic to their plight, to identify with them, that I let go of them and put myself in their place. I was thus not ministering to them. Ministering to myself first of all made me more empathetic. It made me know that in the inner healing ministry, God and his love for the person being healed is important and not the one in the ministry. If God is not Lord of that ministry, then it celebrates what I call a "pity party."

# God Forgives You

## b)   Hoemay's Story

HOEMAY WAS A beautiful little girl, loved by her father. She was truly "daddy's little girl." She looked forward to him coming from work every day so that he would play with her. On weekends, they went out together. She was always riding on his shoulders. Her love for her father was deep.

The relationship between her mother and father deteriorated, and they were finally divorced. Hoemay felt the pain of that separation. Daddy was not coming home anymore. She resented that fact that her mother began dating other men. She developed a very strong resentment for her mother and blamed her for the divorce.

When she was twelve years old, Hoemay began following questionable company. She began to spend much time away from home. First, she began to drink, then went into drugs, and finally, to please her friends, began an active sex life. At the tender age of twelve, she became pregnant, and during one outburst with her mother, she blurted out that she was pregnant. The mother was furious, hurt, disappointed, and concerned that her daughter would give her a new responsibility of taking care of a child. She quickly took her daughter to an abortion clinic, where she had an abortion. The experience was terrible. She blamed her mother for the feeling of being unloved.

Two years later, she became pregnant again and, with her boyfriend, went for an abortion herself. Two days after that procedure, she was in much pain and was rushed to the emergency room, where the doctors removed from her womb arms and legs of the aborted baby. The doctor explained to her that her pregnancy was very far advanced for the kind of abortion procedure that was done. That did not change her for too long. At sixteen years, she was pregnant again, and this time she had her third abortion. The clinic used the vacuum method, and she felt all her insides being taken out of her. She considered this the worst experience of her life.

The Lord led her to a few Catholic youth with whom she began to hang out. She went with them to prayer meetings. At first, it was a place to go to "kill time," but slowly and steadily, the Lord was speaking to her heart.

At one prayer meeting, Hoemay just found herself crying and crying. She could not stop crying. What began with teardrops became a deluge. Many people came to her aid and prayed with her. The inner healing had begun. She began to realize for the first time since her parents separated that she was loved for herself and not for what she had to give. She began to feel the guilt of her past abortions. It was like she was hit by a hurricane—better still, by a tsunami.

It took many months of prayer for Hoemay to be finally freed. It took many visits to her parish priest for the Sacrament of Reconciliation for her to finally experience the forgiveness of God. Today, Hoemay is helping other young women who had had similar experiences. One person she attributed her inner healing to is Mary, the mother of Jesus. Mary knew what it was like to be rejected by Joseph and then by others in her small village. She knew what it was like to see her son rejected, and she is mother of all those who feel rejected and need to be healed from within.

## Let Us Pray

Dear God, reach out to the many Hoemays who are desperate today and would willingly destroy human life for their own emotional satisfaction. Help them and those who encourage them to see the positive light of Jesus and the outstretched arms of the Church calling them to trust you and believe that you love the little children and would help in their care.

Amen.

# You Can Be Renewed

## c)  Whylebert's Story

MANY YEARS AGO, in fact, it was 1974, a few months before my ordination to the priesthood, I was completing a practicum at a large hospital in New York. It was my turn to be on duty, which meant responding to emergencies and helping the injured clients and their families by providing what was then called "therapeutic support."

Around 2:30 a.m., my telephone rang, and I was called to the emergency room. I expected to see someone who had some physical trauma, such as a gunshot wound or a stabbing. In the emergency room, I was too late. The client was already dead. I prayed with and for him as the medical personnel prepared him for the mortuary.

As I was leaving to return to my room, I spoke with one of the police officers involved in the emergency. He told me that another person involved was also at the hospital in another section. After completing my notes, I returned to my room, ready to present the case to the class later that day.

As I presented the case later that day, I paid little attention to what the police officer had shared with me. My only concern in preparing my report for class was the DOA (dead on arrival). My professor picked up on the other victim who was also taken to the hospital and asked about that person. He gave me the responsibility of going to visit that person and to prepare a full report for the class. For some reason, I was not interested in that and made my feelings known to the class. Yet again, my report would not be complete without the whole story to answer the fundamental question, "Why did the man die?"

It took me a few days to visit the living client. For our purpose, I will call him "Whylebert." Whylebert was in the psychiatric section of the hospital, a section I did not like to visit for two reasons: (i) I felt that the clients in that section could be violent at a moment's notice, and (ii) I was identifying too much with them, especially since I had spent much of the previous year studying mental illnesses.

When I visited Whylebert the first time, he was not responsive. He just sat down on the floor in a catatonic state. I left and went to the psychiatric social worker to get some of his history. The history was really frightening to read and made me even more afraid to want to help Whylebert.

Whylebert's past was disturbing and punctuated with violence. As a young child, he witnessed many fights between his father and mother and witnessed his father murdering his mother. He was sent to live with his grandmother, whom he loved very dearly. She went out of her way to show him love, for she saw in Whylebert, her murdered daughter. After living for ten years with his grandmother, he got up one morning to find his grandmother dead. She too had been murdered. He internalized his grief. He was sent to a group home, awaiting foster care. In that home, he slashed one of the male administrators who was speaking with him about his attitude. After a period of years in a detention center, he was placed in a group home. There he murdered one of the attendants, whose body was taken to the hospital.

I was truly afraid for my own safety because Whylebert was quite big and vicious-looking. I did not enter his room. I was too afraid.

At another group discussion, I shared with the class the feelings I felt. I was honest about my fear of Whylebert and wished someone else would take up the case. No one volunteered and "poor" me had to continue or rather begin that case. The program supervisor advised me to do what came naturally. If I felt like fleeing from the case, I should flee. If I felt like trying to look and be fiercer than Whylebert, I should.

For the next four days, I passed Whylebert's room. I looked in but did not dare to enter. I was afraid. My spirit needed to be healed. I needed to be healed of my own fears before I could help others with theirs. I went through two sessions of inner healing or inner cleansing, and from one of these sessions, I understood my fear of Whylebert. There was a fear that I had internalized but never dealt with. That was the moment of true healing for me as I dealt with my own fear and called on Jesus to affirm and strengthen me. I truly identified with Daniel in the lion's den. God's angel will accompany me to Whylebert, whom I considered, at that time, to be a raging beast.

Two weeks had passed, and I entered Whylebert's room. I said, "Hello," but he did not respond. He just looked at me. I could hear my heart pounding in my chest and could feel my saliva drying up as one about to have a panic attack. I held on to the chair in which I was sitting and prayed this prayer:

God, I need you now more than ever to cleanse me from my fear of Whylebert. Give me the words I need now! Now! Now! Now! Dear God.

The words which came from my mouth surprised me. "Whylebert, why don't you stop this s— you are doing? It's about time. I am absolutely tired and fed up with young people throwing up in God's face, after God had blessed them so much."

I think I shocked Whylebert, both by the words I said and the tone with which I said them. He looked me straight in the eyes, like a lion ready to pounce on me. I looked him in the eye, not like the lamb I thought I was, but like an even bigger lion, ready for battle.

After what seemed like staring at each other for eternity, he lowered his gaze. At that moment, I knew I had conquered. In the same stern voice, I began to question Whylebert. He told me his name and shared with me his story. At the end of his story, I asked him, "How does it make you feel?" He turned his head away from me and began to weep and sob. Something was happening to his soul. The Lord had conquered both of us.

In the months that Whylebert remained hospitalized, I visited him on a daily basis. We talked much about his life in the past, about a future of incarceration for the murder he had committed, and about his plans when he would be released in about twenty-five years. More than ever, I led him through inner healing, and although it was difficult for him, we prayed the sinner's prayer and the prayer of forgiveness on more than one occasion.

Whylebert left the hospital and served out his sentence. A few years ago, I was told he was shot to death. Sometimes when I read about young people in violent situations, I think of him. In my own ministry to prisoners, I think of how God had changed Whylebert from a raging bull to a gentle lamb. I think of Whylebert as a frightened young boy, lashing out at adults because adults had hurt him I think of Jesus healing those fears from within and making Whylebert whole again.

We do not purchase hurts and fears from the supermarket. They happen as we go through life, but through the ministry of inner healing, we face those hurts and fears, and God heals us:

> It is no secret what God can do
> What he's done for others, he'll for you,
> With arms wide open, he'll pardon you
> It is no secret what God can do.

The ministry of inner healing must not be confused with mere psychotherapy, for although it uses some of the elements of psychotherapy, it brings Jesus in as the only divine Healer. It allows the person to put their problems and difficulties at the feet of Jesus with the faith that Jesus will supply all that is needed to bring about healing and wholeness.

# PART III

## Shared Reflections

# Called to the Light (1 Pet. 2:9)

THE BIBLE IS God's Word about himself, about us, and about the world and our response to our God. The first observation I made, as I read through "Good News," (Catholic version of the Holy Bible), is the number of times the word "light" is used and the number of times the word "darkness" is used. The authors of the various books of the Bible used the word "light"212 times and the word "darkness" 158 times. I also observed that light and darkness do not complement each other, but that they are opposites. Thus light and darkness cannot or do not exist in the same location.

The Bible begins by telling us that the world was darkness and God spoke to the darkness and created light. He then divided or separated light from the darkness (God also created creatures of the light and made them adaptable to living in the light alone. He also made creatures of the dark, adaptable to living in the dark alone.) Even when God made humanity and made them responsible for all creation, God made them creatures of the day, not of the night (Gen. 1-2). God used darkness as a form of punishment for his creatures of the light. For three days, he sent total darkness to punish Pharaoh and all of Egypt (Exod. 10:22). God also put darkness between the Hebrew people and the Egyptians when they called out to him (Josh. 24:7).

One sees from the perspective of the Bible that darkness stands for anything opposed to God. It is also a punishment from God on those who live and were born of and for the light. Psalm 18:28 says, "O God, you turn my darkness into light." Psalm 88:12 says, "You have made even my closest friends abandon me, and darkness is my only companion."

As humanity continued to walk the route of darkness, their desire was always for the light. The prophet Isaiah prophesied, "The people that walk in darkness have seen a great light . . ." (Isa. 9:2). "I will turn darkness into light before them" (Isa. 42:16). Jeremiah, on the other hand, sees what God will do to the enemy of Israel. "They will be banished to darkness" (Jer. 23:12). In Ezekiel 32:8, the Lord says of Egypt, "I will plunge your world in darkness."

The theme of darkness as a punishment from God also plays out in the New Testament. The New Testament gives hope from darkness to light. "The people that walked in darkness have seen a great light" (Matt. 4:16). "A light that shines in the darkness and the darkness could not over power it" (John 1:5). "Let us put aside the work of darkness and put on the armor of light" (Rom. 13:12). "God is light in him there is no darkness" (1 John 1:5). Although the New Testament continues the theme of darkness as punishment, the emphasis is more on hope. God will change darkness into light.

# Church in Darkness

I HAD COMPLETED a mission at a local parish, and my subtheme on the final day was "God is doing a new thing in a new season." Over the past years, God has been purging his Church. He has been allowing his light to shine on the darkness in this Church, for as the Word affirms, "All that is done in darkness will come out into the light." We felt that the Church was going through a period of darkness. It certainly was. Year after year, the Church was under attack. God had to test out the strength and our resolve. He promised to be always with his Church.

Did you notice that every Lenten season, the Church was under attack? The clergy sexual abuse scandals, the DaVinci code, the so-called archeological findings of the tomb and bones of Jesus, and the so-called discovery of the gospel of Judas all shook the very foundations of our belief. Yet God said to his Church, "I am doing a new thing in a new season" (Isa. 43:28). Again God says, "I will turn darkness into light before them" (Isa. 42:16) and again in Matthew 4:16, "The people that once walked in darkness are seeing a new light."

# The Light Has Come

GOD IS CERTAINLY doing a new thing in this new season as he has done in the past. The world and the Church have had seven years of distress. We have seen the war in Iraq and Afghanistan, the ethnic cleansing between the Hotoors and the Tootsies in Africa, the terrible tsunami in Asia, the almost destruction of Louisiana by a hurricane, etc. Those past seven years have been testing years for the Church and for the world.

God is doing a new thing in this new season. It was on the eighth day that the Holy Spirit came down upon the Church to begin the new evangelization. It was on the eighth day that all males were circumcised as a sign that they belong to God (Gen. 7). It was on the eighth time around Jericho that the walls came tumbling down. It was only after the seven last words on the cross that Jesus dies and rose from the dead. It was during his seventeenth year that Joseph began his journey into grief, disappointment, and sadness before he knew the joy and satisfaction of the light from his eighteenth year onward. It was God who said to Moses, "Give me your first born sons. Give me the first born from your cattle . . . etc." (Exod. 22:30-66) When I look at the beatitudes, the seventh deal with generalities and the eighth deal specifically with the person. "Blessed are you when people abuse you and persecute you, etc . . ." (Matt. 5). What God is really doing in this new time and in this new season is guiding his Church from darkness into light.

The letter of St. Peter from whom the quotation for this presentation was taken was written to us, God's chosen people, "who live as refugees scattered throughout the provinces" (1 Pet. 1:1).

# Sons and Daughters of Light

THAT'S US, THE sons and daughters of those brought from Africa. God chose our fore-parents for life in the diaspora. We can look at all the negative effects of the slave trade and of slavery, we can talk about what we lost, but can we also talk about what we have gained through our free acceptance of Jesus Christ as our personal Lord and Savior.

True, through the institution of slavery, we lost what is fundamental to every civilization—that is its culture as expressed through its religion, its family system, and its folklore and its folkways expressed in its songs and stories, but we gained the ability to call God, "God" and share our oneness with God through our Negro spirituals. That was our binding force as we faced the uncertainties of another tomorrow.

Peter reminds us that just as gold is tested by fire, the faith of the African was tested by physical slavery and continues to be tested as we daily throw off the new shackles that are ever near, ready to put us in a new moral slavery. Through this test, our faith endures (1 Pet. 1:7).

The Lord is calling us to enter with him into this time, "the fullness of time" (Gal. 5:4) and into the new season (Isa. 43:19). God is saying to the Church today, "Go out of the city and build a road for your returning people. Prepare a highway, clear it of stones . . ." (Isa. 62:10).

This is the age of evangelization, an age of proclaiming the gospel not only in words, but in action. This is the age when the Lord is calling on the children of Africa in the diaspora to stop living in the past with its stories of hate and dehumanization. God has called us out of that darkness—he has taken us to the mountain top—we have witnessed his transfiguration, and he sends us back in the valley of dry bones (Ezek. 51:1-7) to command that God's army begins to live again, looking forward, ever forward, to the new thing that he is using us to do and to be.

Do not for one minute believe that I want to erase the facts of history. I certainly do not, but I want to move us from the then to the now to the tomorrow. For if we remain in yesterday, today will never be a reality and tomorrow will never exist. God has called us from the darkness, sadness, and dehumanization of our history to a new time—a time of true freedom, a time which makes us see the "promised land" together and gives us the courage to enter it together because God has always been, is, and will always be with us. "Life," he said to Moses in Exodus 3, "I have seen your suffering, I have heard your cry, and I am doing something about it. I am calling you out of darkness into my wonderful light."

# Jesus, My Friend

"IN THE PAST God spoke to our ancestors many times and in many ways through the prophets, but in these last days he has spoken to us through his Son. He is the one through whom God created the universe, the one whom God has chosen to possess all things at the end. He reflects the brightness of God's glory and is the exact likeness of God's own being, sustaining the universe with his powerful word. After achieving forgiveness for the sins of mankind, he sat down in heaven at the right side of God, the Supreme Power . . ." (Heb. 1:1-3).

I want to share with you these few words—words of challenge, words of affirmation, words of faith, words of hope, and words from God. These words are words that will make us recognize and realize the tremendous love that God has for each person and for all people, a love for the sinner and for the saint, love for the obedient and the disobedient. In fact, as long as we are persons, God loves us. John 3:16, a favorite passage, says, "God loves the world so much that he gave his only begotten Son, so that anyone who believes in him would not perish, but would have everlasting life . . ." Too often, we feel or think that God only loves perfection and that the more perfect we are the more God loves us. To hold that opinion would make God's love exclusive, but God's love is an all-inclusive love, hence the deep significance of Good Friday,

Easter Sunday, and Pentecost. They are all liturgical expressions of God's love for everyone.

Let us look first at the Good Friday experience. The Son of God, the perfection of all perfections—the Word made flesh—was crucified between two criminals. One imperfect criminal pleads with Jesus, "Lord, remember me when you come into your kingdom . . ." To which Jesus replies, "Today you will be with me in paradise . . ." The most important phrase in the dialogue with Jesus and the criminal is "with me." Perfect love is always a love that wants to share. Thus Jesus does not say, "Today I will send you to paradise," rather, "Today you will be with me in paradise." We can look at the Resurrection as recorded in Luke 24:15-35, especially verse 38, "Wasn't it like a fire burning within us when he talked to us . . ." Love is truly like a fire burning within us, for when we stand before love, all our unloving ways, thoughts, and actions are burnt in the fires of that pure love, and we become forever changed. The fire of that pure love also rained down at Pentecost and consumed all those in the upper room to the extent that they left the upper room different. They were able to preach because they were affirmed by pure love. They were able to dispel their fears because in the presence of perfect love, all fears disappear. The presence of that love inflamed the listeners with so much love that love made them hear the words in their own native language (Acts 2).

The quotation with which I began this presentation shows us that love—that pure love, that perfect love—was revealed to our ancestors through the prophets. Even before the period of prophets, that love was revealed to Moses as he stood before the burning bush of God's love. He had to take off his shoes, and not only was he forever changed but also others were changed as he radiated that love from within to without him. He thus became a spokesman of love.

Isaiah experienced the cleansing power of that love when one of the seraphs took burning coal and touched his lips saying to him, "Your iniquity is cleansed and your guilt is purged . . ." (Isa. 6:6). In fact, I can continue going through the scriptures, drawing out example after example of God's pure love for each and every person. But that love is not enclosed or entrapped in the Bible. It is real, it is true, it is today. It is a love that has been revealed time and time again. It is a love that is real, that is physical, that is intellectual, and that affects our emotions. It is an affection of the heart. There is no love that affects only the mind. The heart is and will always remain the seat of love. To use the words of songs made popular by Carey Landry, "The only love we ever keep is what we give away . . ." How true is that expression when we apply it to God's love. "God loves the world so much that he did spare his own son, but gave him up to benefit us all . . ." "God is love, and anyone who lives in love, lives in God and God lives in them . . ." Can you imagine that love transforms us from being merely human to being divine, for when God lives in us through love, the fire of that love transforms us and carries us into the realm of divinity? Praise God.

Throughout the history of our Church, God's Church, God has expressed that love through his Son and in the Holy Spirit. God has also expressed his love for us through the Holy Eucharist, for Jesus himself said, "Anyone who eats my flesh and drinks my blood, lives in me and I live in him . . . and I will raise him up on the last day . . ." What love has Jesus given us in the Eucharist—he will personally raise us up on the last day.

Why? Because we have accepted his love and have decided to give his love away.

We must be aware that love is not a cushy-cushy, only emotional experience. Love is a rational decision based on one's own experience of God's love. We sometimes have to ask the question, "Why does God love me, wretched as I am?" The answer which ought to come to us is, "God loves me because I am loveable. God loves me because he made me out of love. God loves me because God is love." Having experienced that love, I cannot but share that love. I cannot keep it. The more I give love, the more I receive love; the more affirmed I become, the more my faith challenges me to give more love until like Jesus, I can say, "I thirst." "It is finished."

Let us go to the seventeenth century. In the years 1647-1690, a simple religious woman Margaret Mary Alacoque was on fire with God's love, not because she was religious, but because she had experienced God's love. It was that experience which led her to live a life in love, to spend time before the Blessed Sacrament, glowing in the sunshine of God's love through Jesus. Jesus appeared to her during the octave of Corpus Christi (1675). Jesus again expressed his love for all people. He also expressed sadness over the indifference of people to his love. The devotion—Eucharistic devotion of the Sacred Heart of Jesus—the devotion to God's love began in earnest in the church. St. John Eudes (1601-1680) stated, "The Divine Heart of Jesus is a furnace of love before our gaze in the Most Holy Sacrament . . ."

In 1879, the first Confraternity of the Eucharistic Heart of Jesus was established, and in 1883, it received approbation from Pope Leo XIII. The establishment of that confraternity is 123 years old, and one ought to ask oneself, "To what extent is there more love among you? To what extent has your faith in God allowed you to be in love with God? To what extent has the fire of God's love burned out the doubts, fears, anxieties, and frustrations from your life? To what extent are you able, capable, and willing, and in fact, are spreading the devotion to God's love through Jesus Christ? To what extent does God's love lead you to appreciate God's mercy as St. Faustina has shown us through the revelations she has received from Jesus? To what extent are we willing, able, and have made a decision to love in spite of everything? To what extent are we saying from a heart of love, 'My God, I trust in you'?"

Our times are indeed both troubled and troubling. The scandals which the media is exploding is troubling both clergy and people, since those scandals do not originate from outside the Church but from within the Church itself. They are not attacks on the church from outsiders, but they are attacks within the church. A virus that has infiltrated the very heart of the church—the priesthood—is a scandal, which is affecting those ordained to celebrate the Eucharist—the sacrament of love. It is a virus that attacks love. It is a virus that attacks the very heart of our faith. Yet Jesus will triumph, for he has given us the vaccination against that virus. Do you know what that vaccination is or how it ought to be prepared? I will tell you. Take

4 cc of faith,

4 cc of hope,

25 cc of love.

Mix them together, adding a full glass of prayer, intercession, and sacrifice.

Using the clean syringe of the Sacred Heart of Jesus (that syringe is our apostolic desire to spread devotion to the Sacred Heart) and inject the Church. Only one vaccination is needed. The effects will be instantaneous, and the healing process will begin. Remember, we must not compromise or be cheap with the love, nor must we dilute the mixture with doubt, anger, and suspicion. Remember, the greatest gift we ever keep is what we give away. We are not only to share and spread his love but to be his love for others.

# The New Garment—(Isa. 4:10)

THE STORY IS told of a grocer who had a problem with thieves breaking into his grocery shop. He used all modern electronic devices to catch the thief, but that thief always outsmarted him. Finally, the grocer decided to spread fresh cement all around the shop before he closed for the night. Sure enough, the thief came. The police had little trouble in apprehending him, because he left "footprints."

Henry Wardsworth Longfellow, in his poem "The Song of Life" wrote, "Lives of great men all remind us, we can make our lives sublime, and departing leave behind us footprints on the sands of time." A beautiful verse made popular a few years ago entitled, "Footprints" read:

A man had a dream one night. In his dream he was walking along the beach with the Lord. As they walked, visions from the man's life flowed across the sky. When he looked down, he saw two sets of footprints etched in the sand. One set belonged to him and the other set belonged to the Lord. As he continued to walk, he noticed that at the saddest and most trying times of his life, there was only one set of footprints in the sand. He asked the Lord, "When I needed you most, why did you leave me?"

"My son, my precious child," replied the Lord, "I would never leave you. During those times of trial and suffering, when you saw only one set of footprints . . . That was the time I carried you."

70

The Book of Ecclesiastes, Chapter 3, says very clearly: "There is nothing new under the sun. God has created for us a beautiful world." The Bible tells us that God took five days to create that world of perfection.

*Everything was good.*

*The trees were clothed in their garments of green and brown, the sun was clothed in its bright yellow, the seas and oceans were clothed in their many shades of green, the sky was clothed in its many shades of blue, the clouds were clothed in their cottony white, the moon large and bright on the evening sky. Each animal came fully clothed in only one garment which with time was recycled. On the sixth day God made man and woman. They were not clothed.*

The Bible tells us that they were naked—a fact that they did not realize until sin entered their lives. Genesis 3:10 says, "He (the man) answered, 'I heard you in the garden and hid from you because I was naked.'"

The first garment for humanity was not made by God but by man and woman themselves. "As soon as they had eaten it, they were given understanding and realized that they were naked, so they sewed fig leaves together and covered themselves . . ." (Gen. 3:7).

A garment, says the biblical lexicon, is an article of clothing to cover oneself. A garment is either made or purchased. It is usually tailor made so that it fits and covers all the parts of the body. We wear garments today for a number of reasons such as

(i) we will not be arrested for indecent exposure, (ii) to maintain a healthy body temperature—when it is hot, we wear less clothing, and when it is cold, we cover up, (iii) to look and feel good. I have met some persons who say to me that they prefer the winter weather because the winter garments look better. Apart from the reasons for wearing garments, we also wear different garments for different occasions, e.g., we wear (1) sleeping garments, (2) at-home garments, (3) party garments, (4) church garments, (5) wedding garments, (6) baptism garments, (7) First Communion garments, (8) confirmation garments, etc. We are the only ones, since God's creation, who change as many garments in one year. We are even trying to give our style of garments to the animals. Just see the movie *Beverly Hills Chihuahua* and see how we attempt to humanize everything.

In Genesis, Chapter 3 is a pivotal chapter in the history of God's association with humanity of humanity's sin, God's punishment, and the naming of the woman by the man. Until now, she was only called "woman" and the man, "man." Now the man is called Adam (all humanity) and the woman (Eve, mother of all that lives).

In Genesis 3:21, we read that God himself clothes Adam and Eve with animal skins, "and the Lord made garments from animal skins for Adam and Eve."

The term "garment" appears seventy-three times in the Good News Bible under two large headings (1) garments of righteousness and (2) heavenly garments. We shall say no more about this today. All we shall do is peep at the baptism liturgy, especially the new baptism liturgy. After the infant is baptized and anointed with the consecrated chrism, the church gives a white (clean) garment to the child. The priest says, "You have become a new creation and have clothed yourself with Christ. See in this white garment an outward sign of your Christian dignity. With your family and friends to help you by word and example, bring that dignity unspoilt into the everlasting life of heaven." Again at the burial service of a Catholic, the coffin is draped with a white pall. The priest says, "On the day of his/her baptism, our brother/sister put on Christ (white garment). On the day of Christ's coming, may he/she be clothed in glory."

That white (clean) garment given at baptism is really the garment of righteousness, which should be kept unstained until resurrection. That white (clean) garment becomes for us the garment of glory. As the book of Revelation relates, "These are those who have kept their robes clean." Revelation 22:14 says, "Happy are those who wash their robes clean and so have the right to eat the fruit from the tree of life and go through the gates of the city."

For the next few days, we will be continuing our reflection on this garment of salvation, but for now, let us return to the beginning of this opportunity and privilege to do, let us remember that the footprints we leave behind can build or destroy others. When we finally leave this world, we and God will be looking at the footprints we left behind. Let us listen now to the best poem.

# MISCELLANEOUS PRAYERS

# Thank You, Lord

LORD, IN THE many years of priesthood, you have allowed me, and the many positions of responsibility you have allowed me. I too, in my enthusiasm to share your love with others, have been the cause of hurt to others, as others have been the cause of hurt for me. Help me to forgive all those who have hurt me in word and deed, and help those whom I have hurt to find forgiveness in God's love, holiness, and goodness. Mary, Mother of love and St. Joseph, help all find healing in the same love you have for Jesus, who is Lord, forever and ever. Amen.

# Prayer of Healing

O LORD JESUS Christ, out of love you died and rose for me and gave me the Holy Spirit. In his light and through the prayers of your holy mother, proclaim the gospel of your love in my heart and in my life today. I renounce attachment to sin, and I rebuke in your name every spirit of evil and disorder. Let your risen glory shine all through me that I may love and adore you with my whole being. Shine in my body, my brain, nervous system, my chemistry, every tissue, and organ. Shine in my mind and will and all their powers in my psyche, my unconscious, my sexuality, and all my energies so that I may love, work, pray, play, and sleep in your holiness. Shine in my heart and spirit. Put to death my egotism. Cast out my fear and every sinful habit. Enlighten me wholly, and transform all my relationships. Fully restore your image in me so that I no longer live, but you live in me. Root me and center me in the Father's love. Consecrate me to his praise and to the wholehearted love of my brothers and sisters, and order all my days and deeds in your peace, for you are my life, my hope, my joy, and my healing. I send up glory to you and your eternal father, together with your all-holy, good, and life-giving Spirit, now and always and forever and ever. Amen.

# Sinner's Prayer

MY GOD, I come before you a sinner, still able to call you Abba, since I received you at baptism and have become your child. I know that many things in my life are against your commands, both those things that I am conscious of and those that I am not conscious of. I beg pardon for attitudes that I have developed over the years which have helped me to cope with the strains of life.

Father, those attitudes, I have always considered normal, yet, I know they are not. I have, over the years, developed attitudes of selfishness, both to things and to persons.

Father, for the many times I have been dishonest, I beg your forgiveness. Father, for the many times I have pretended to be what I am not, I ask your forgiveness. Father, for the many times I have allowed the flesh to be greater than the spirit, I ask your forgiveness.

And now, Father, I make a true and honest confession of all my sins (pause), and I pray that the prayer of the Church gathered here will give me the strength and courage to live a life worthy of you. I ask this Father, in the name of your Son, Jesus, who lives with you and the Holy Spirit forever. Amen.

# Prayer of Inner Healing

DEAR GOD, FATHER of our Lord and Savior Jesus Christ and Father of us all gathered in his name, the God of Abraham, Isaac, Jacob, the God of my faith-filled parents and grandparents, I am in your presence, once again asking for healing. I am begging you, Lord, to heal me from whatever hurts I have carried and am carrying with me from the moment of my conception until now.

Perhaps, Lord, my coming into the world was not a pleasant experience for my parents. Thus, Lord, I was not as welcomed as I should have been. I ask you, Lord, to heal me of all senses of rejection that I experienced as I was growing in my mother's womb. Perhaps too, Lord, many attempts were made to abort me, but your strength saw me through those difficult, fearful, and anxious months in my mother's womb. Lord, reach out and heal me.

Thank you, Lord, for allowing me to see the light of day in your world. Lord, I pray a healing for the many times I was made to feel unwanted, for the many times I did not live up to what my parents wanted. Perhaps my mother wanted a boy and had a girl, or wanted a girl and had a boy. Lord, I pray for a healing of that moment in my life.

Lord, reach into the significant moments of life and heal whatever negative influences affected me. Reach, Lord, in the negative experiences I had in school with my teachers and other students. Forgive me for those feelings of resentment I had for that particular teacher whom I disliked for the way she treated me, for the times she called me "good for nothing" and rushed me to be a failure in life. Forgive me for that particular student who avoided me and never allowed me to be part of a circle of friends. Thank you, Lord, praise your holy name.

Lord, reach out to my working years, the employer who used and abused me, who failed to pay me a just wage and who always threatened to fire me. Lord, I really tried to be a friend to that employer. I accepted all the insults and intimidations just to keep employment. Lord, for the coworkers whom I reported to be in the bosses' "good books," Lord, I am so sorry for those employers who suffered because of me and made me suffer.

Lord, please heal all the negative forces that attached themselves to my mature years. The poor choices I made for a spouse, for the suffering I caused my spouse, and for the suffering my spouse caused me. Lord, please forgive me and heal my children, for my failure to accept them as my own and for my failure to provide the material, spiritual, and economic needs. Lord, heal them right now, as only you can. Lord, forgive me.

Whatever stage I am in life, Lord, I beg for your healing. Clean me, Lord, and remove from me all the scars left by my past. Take that spiritual sandpaper and smooth over those scars. I know,

Lord, the process may be painful, but I need to be whole—to be free to praise you with all my heart.

Lord, I praise you, I thank you, and I glorify you.

Even now, Lord, O right now, Lord,
Send us love, send us power, send us grace.
Even now, Lord, O right now, Lord,
    Let the warmth of your presence fill our hearts.

# Epilogue

Dear God, my life has so far

Been a true celebration

Of your love for all.

As I walk with you

Through the remaining years,

Let me share that

Celebration with others

So that others will

Experience the

Endless Celebration of Life.

# Index

Edwards Brothers, Inc.
Thorofare, NJ  USA
November 21, 2011